YOUR KNOWLEDGE HAS VALUE

- We will publish your bachelor's and master's thesis, essays and papers

- Your own eBook and book - sold worldwide in all relevant shops

- Earn money with each sale

Upload your text at www.GRIN.com and publish for free

Bibliographic information published by the German National Library:

The German National Library lists this publication in the National Bibliography; detailed bibliographic data are available on the Internet at http://dnb.dnb.de .

Imprint:

Copyright © 2010 GRIN Verlag, Open Publishing GmbH
Print and binding: Books on Demand GmbH, Norderstedt Germany
ISBN: 978-3-668-18505-0

This book at GRIN:

http://www.grin.com/en/e-book/318987/logic-and-effects-of-rational-ignorance-the-theory-of-public-choice

Rodrigue Bienvenue Nanfack

Logic and Effects of Rational Ignorance. The Theory of Public Choice

GRIN Publishing

GRIN - Your knowledge has value

Since its foundation in 1998, GRIN has specialized in publishing academic texts by students, college teachers and other academics as e-book and printed book. The website www.grin.com is an ideal platform for presenting term papers, final papers, scientific essays, dissertations and specialist books.

Visit us on the internet:

http://www.grin.com/

http://www.facebook.com/grincom

http://www.twitter.com/grin_com

Seminararbeit

WWU

SS2010

Rodrigue Bienvenue Nanfack

Rational Ignorance

Westfälische Wilhelms-Universität Münster - George Mason University
Faculty of Economical Sciences
Center for Interdisciplinary Economics (CIW)
Lecture: Theory of Public Choice

Course of Studies: Politics and
Economy

Contents

1. Introduction

Many political failure arguments implicitly assume that voters are irrational (Wittmann 1995, 1989; Coate and Morris 1995). The main resonance of this paper going to show that this assumption is plausible. This paper will show, why voters prefer to be ignorant, what logic is behind this behavior, what effects this ignorance could or may have in the election result. The Problematic of this paper is try to understand what issue may those behavior bring to election system and try to demonstrate what is properly RATIONAL ignorance?. Josh Billings (in Caruth and Ehrlich 1988, P.205) said "The trouble with people is not that they don´t know, but that they know so much that they ain´t so"; argued to this citation, we could conclude, that the RATIONAL ignorance is not because of failed information, but because voluntary refuse being informed. The subject person won´t being informed, because he doesn't see any utilization of this information for him. The RATIONAL ignorance occurs when the cost of educating oneself on an issue exceeds the potential benefit that the knowledge would provide. Rational ignorance can be most funding in general elections case, where the voter see probability his vote to change the outcome as pretty small. Those voters will definitely not go to vote.

Bryan Caplan has theorized that voters anomalous beliefs cannot be attributed solely to rational ignorance, he states that irrational systemic bias is also at work (Caplan Bryan, 2003). To make concrete, what do rational ignorance mean, we will use one example of *ingrimayne* at this level to make clear how rational ignorance could get manifested: The Government has new policy that involve major sums of money (Tax money). For example a weapons industry (defense department) can cost $50 Billion. This amounts to about $200 for every person in the United States, or $1000 for family of five. Yet few people spend much time studying these policies. A reason is that to understand them requires many hours of study and the probability that an understanding of them will change them in any way are very small. Thus, for most citizens the benefit of leaning about program that does not directly affect them is small, the cost is large and they end up not knowing much about the program, those poorly informed citizens are called by economist "rational ignorant"

We cannot analyze the rational ignorance, without analyze the fiscal Illusion, because that behavior could practically allow politics to misuse their power, or oriented policies in that way that citizen's couldn´t follow and understand them. In their book Democracy in Deficit (1977) James M. Buchanan and Richard E. Wagner suggest that the complicated nature of the U.S. tax system causes fiscal illusion and results in greater public expenditure than would be the case in an idealized system in which everyone is aware in detail of what their share of the costs of government is. We could than define fiscal illusion as a situation when government revenue are unobserved by taxpayers then the cost of government is perceived to be less expensive than it actually is.

The next part of this paper will try first to show the logic and effect of rational ignorance in the political process, the second part will than try to show how might politicians attempt to use rational ignorance to promote their interest, and this part will be following by the part, which will show the limit on the extent to which voter ignorance can be exploited and before conclude, we will that discuss about policies that might reduce fiscal illusion.

2. Logic and effects of rational ignorance

On this part of paper, we will try to show how rational, rational ignorance could be, what that logic is and what effect this rationality could have. In case of Votes, voters are confronted with incentives and at the end the factor, which play a really biggest role is the self-interest. Like in the market consumers will only apply for products they need and will not try to get information concerning other products. Concerning the homo economicus model, voters or people will just care about information that brings them some incentives.... Information that does not affect their private interest will be neglected and they are in that case totally ignorant, but in the rationality.

The origin of rational ignorance or ration irrationality come from sources of believes preference. And to understand what this mean we should try to answer this question "why do people prefer to believe some things that are not true or not supported by the evidence?" "What kind of irrational preferences do we have?" The properly answer of this questions going to be non scientific answer, because they are no studies, that support this.

The first answer is a self-interested bias that support that people tend to hold political belief that, if generally accepted, would benefit themselves or the group they identify with. That means the reasons of rational ignorance of the conservative republican and that from the democrat will be completely different. The same reason will apply by people from different social level, independent of their level of education.

The second answer is the Belief as self-image constructor, people prefer to hold political beliefs that best fit with the image of themselves that they want to adopt and project. For example, people that portray themselves as a compassionate, generous person will definitely have voted for Obama in 2008.

The third answer will be a belief of coherence bias; people are biased towards beliefs that fit well with their existing belief. In one sense, of course, the tendency to prefer belief that well with an existing belief system is rational, rather than a bias. But this tendency can also function as a bias. For instance, there are many people who believe capital punishment deters crime and many who believe it doesn't; there are also many who believe that innocent people are frequently convicted and many who believe that they aren't. But there are relatively few people who think both that capital punishment deters crime, and that many innocent people are convicted. Likewise, few people think capital punishment fails to deter crime, but few innocent people are convicted. In other words, people will tend to either adopt both of the factual beliefs that would tend to support capital punishment, or adopt both of the factual beliefs that would tend to undermine capital punishment. On a similar note, relatively few people believe that drug use is extremely harmful to society but that laws against drugs are and will remain ineffective. Yet, a priori, there's no reason why those positions (i.e., positions in which a reason for a particular policy and a reason against that policy both have a sound factual basis) should be less probable than the positions we actually find to be prevalent (i.e., positions according to which all or most of the relevant considerations point in the same direction).

The forth answer is beliefs as tools of social bonding; People prefer to hold the political beliefs of other people they like and want to associate with. It is extremely unlikely that a person who doesn't like most conservatives would ever convert to conservative beliefs. Relatedly, the physical attractiveness of people influences others' tendency to agree with them politically. A study of Canadian federal elections found that attractive candidates received more than two and a half times as many votes as unattractive candidates—although most voters surveyed denied in the strongest possible terms that physical attractiveness had any influence on their votes.

Based on the information from *spryne*t we could than better understand where the origins of rational ignorance or rational irrationality are. The next part of this work will more try to show what logic is to understand under this rational ignorance. The causes, that may push people to decide being rational ignorant or rational irrationally.

2.1. Logic under rational ignorance model

To understand what the logic of Rational ignorance is, we should first try to explain why some ignorance can be rational and what is that mean. Like said in our introduction, the logic of being rational ignorant is only that the person won´t apply for information, because the information is not important for him or uninteresting for his goal or the i9nformation is more costly as his benefit. The logic is that, the cost of apply for those information are higher than benefit. The rational voter is interested only in information which might or could change his preliminary voting decision.

First, a related theory. The theory of rational ignorance say that people often choose to been irrational (rational irrationality) because the costs of collecting information are greater than the expected value of the information. This truly apply for politic information. For example if we ask political student of the University of Münster who is their deputy in the regional parliament in Düsseldorf or in national Parliament in Berlin (Bundestag), most of them won´t know, because not because they are completely ignorant, but only because this information is pretty uninteresting for their goal or costly to them as a benefit this information will bring to them. That is the same when you ask many Germans about where Germany apply his Gas, mostly of them won´t be able to answer the question because they don´t have information about the origin of the gay they use to warm themselves in the winter. We can understand why people won´t apply for some information, because if you tried to keep track of every politician and bureaucrat who is supposed to be representing or serving you, you´d probably spend your whole life on that. You could probably know who you will vote by the next election, but the probability that your vote make the decision is so small and uncertain, because the other 900 000 voters in your district are still going to vote for whomever they were going to vote for before you collected the information.

The similar cases also apply on the theory of rational irrationality that say that people often choose rationally to adopt irrationality beliefs because the cost of rational beliefs exceeds their benefits.

Sprynet define two kind of rationalities: *Instrumental rationality* (or "means-end rationality") and *Epistemic rationality*. Instrumental rationality consists in choosing the correct means to attain one´s actual goals, given one´s actual beliefs. This is the kind of rationality that economists generally assume in explaining human behavior. Epistemic rationality consist, roughly, in forming beliefs in truth-conductive ways, accepting beliefs that well-supported by evidence, avoiding logical fallacies, avoiding contradictions, revising one´s beliefs in the light of new evidence against them, and so on. From this definitions we don´t understand that people often think illogically because it is in their own interests to do so. This is particularly is typically the case of political beliefs. According to Caplan´s examples: If I believe, irrationally, that immigrants are no good at running convenience marts, I bear the costs of this belief; e.g., I may wind up paying more or traveling farther for goods I want. But if I believe (also irrationally) that immigrants are harming the American economy in general, I bear virtually none of the costs of this belief. There is a tiny chance that my belief may have some effect on public policy; if so, the cost will borne by society as a whole (and particularly immigrants); only a negligible portion of it will be borne by me personally. For this reason, I have an incentive to be more rational about immigrants´ ability to run convenience marts than I am about immigrants´ general effects on society. In general, just as I receive virtually none of the benefit of my collecting of political information, so I receive virtually none of the benefit of my thinking rationally about political issues.

Theory, Caplan writes Information is a good like any other. The primary benefit of information is that it reduces the probability of acting in false beliefs; the primary cost is that acquiring information requires time. Basic microeconomics predicts that (ignoring risk-aversion) individuals acquire information up to the point where the expected marginal benefits equal the expected marginal costs (Stigler 1961). Caplan also argued that, beyond that point, acquiring information becomes selfishly counter-productive; while you will avoid more mistakes, it is on balance cheaper to commit them. If marginal benefits of information are zero, the rational economic decision (homo economicus) is to be ignorant. If the Mmarket pays nothing for knowledge of ancient Egypt, there is no reason to spend time learning about it (Caplan, Bryan, 1999) "rational ignorant" always refers to everyone, who may little know or nothing, because expected benefits of knowledge are negligible for him. The rational ignorance or rational irrationality can be demonstrated by empirical study and to proof that we will use a Caplan Example: Suppose that spending one more hour learning about politician voting records allows you to shift your vote to a candidate whose policies, if adopted, would be $100 better for you. The expected marginal benefit of an hour of study is emphatically not $100, but $100 multiplied by the probability that you cast the decisive vote, tipping an otherwise deadlocked outcome. In virtually any real-world election, that probability will be essentially zero, implying an expected marginal benefit of zero as well (Olson 1965; Downs 1957), this problem of imperfect information matters more in politics than market, because on the market, consumers are not omniscient, but can use a clear incentives to understand, if a merchandise price is worth the asking price. To better understanding that problem of incentive estimation we could better refer on this diagram billow:

DIAGRAM 1: Incentives and Estimation

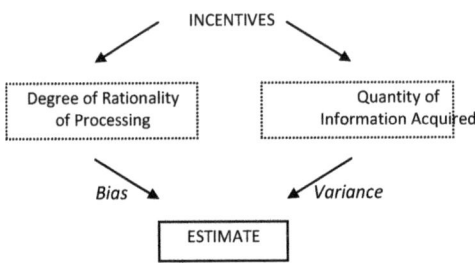

Compared to the ignorant voter, market ignorant is basically not ignorant; he is ignorant of details of the Marketplace, not its basics. The voters have any incentive to study and learn about the basics of politics. We should say at this place that this is not completely true, because everyone know something about politics; nevertheless empirical studies inform us that people (citizens) are more ignorant in politics than in the marketplace, and that form of ignorance is shocking. So we could keep at this way that rational ignorance is a phenomena, that exist and the reason is must basing on information. Information cost made prefer being irrational, and that rational ignorance is rational irrationality.

Diagram 1: Rational Ignorant

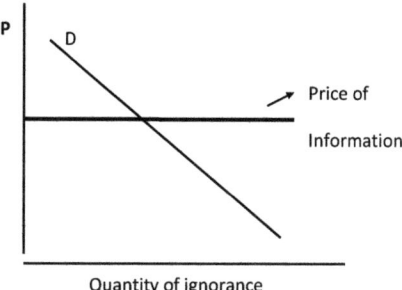

Quantity of ignorance

Benefits – Costs < 0 (Say Downs, for most people) Note voting costs and information costs both exist. Given this information about Costs and Benefits, Down argues that nearly all citizens should adopt a strategy of "Rational Ignorance". The next part of this paper will try to the effect of rational ignorance that means the consequence of this practice.

2.2. Effects of rational ignorance

Rational Ignorance may also have some consequences or effect in the society, particularly on the politics. If citizens and voters do not have any idea about politics and policies, politicians could than safely cater to the special interest, that make their business, like vote new policies, that support them and their partners, policies, that are not on the public interest. This situation often named "concentrated benefits diffuse costs." The profits by those situations gone to some special Interest, but the average voter may be disadvantaged from those patterns. The beneficiaries may mostly being lobbyist. No voter, therefore, will bother to even learn of existence of the legislation, but its beneficiaries may well employ a full-time staff of lobbyist to protect their livelihood. (Olson 1965, Weingast et al 1981; Rowley et al 1988; Magee et al 1989). The relation between rational ignorance and special interest is that, special interest like weapon industry or economy can use their money to buy politicians support. They finance politicians campaign and because of voters ration ignorance, politicians will that support those private or special interest by making policy that support those special interest. Voters' won´t see that, because he don´t have information about the situation. In equilibrium, of course, politicians have to strike a balance between special Interest and voter interests, but the less informed the voters are, the less their interest count. (Grossman and Helpman 1994)

To better show how concrete the effect of rational ignorance are, Bryan Caplan use two Arguments: Suppose that only 10% of voters are well-informed; they vote for the candidate who puts more weight on voter welfare. The remaining 90% are completely uninformed and vote by flipping a coin. Common sense says that this situation is hopeless. Basic statistics, however, implies that as the size of the electorate increases, the randomness of individual voters matters less and less. In percentage terms, errors tend to cancel each other out. In fact, for a reasonably large electorate, we can practically guarantee that in a two-party race, each candidate gets half of the uninformed vote. No matter what a candidate does, he gets at least 45% of the vote. To win, though, a candidate needs more; and the only way to get more is to court the informed voters. What fraction of the well-informed does a politician need to win? 51%. In other words, whichever candidate *the majority of well-informed voters prefers* wins the election, even though by assumption the well-informed are out-numbered 9:1.

A parallel argument holds for ignorance about policy. Suppose that most voters are ignorant about International economics. As long as this ignorance leads equal fractions of voters to over- or under-estimate the benefits of free trade, the equilibrium policy remains the same. Voter ignorance by itself therefore does not imply that protectionism prevails. As long as errors are random rather than systematic, and the electorate is large, an ignorant electorate acts "as if" it were fully informed.

Uninformed citizen (beliefs) can be rational: Minimal information leads to large mean absolute measurement error, but not bias. (Caplan, 1999) the most consequence of rational ignorance in election case is that voters will get lied by politician. The lost control and they are not able to see what happen in the government. The most famous consequence of rational ignorance is that voters help interest group to promote their own interest. Because parties need money to promote image, interest groups supply that money to them and after win election, those parties will than support any policies favorable to that interest groups (sponsors). For them the cost/benefit calculation is positive. Interest groups can even give large sums if they can reasonable expect to get more back from the parties once they are in power (and they can). For most groups Benefits > Cost even for what most of us would think of as high costs. The result of that behavior is that voters are duped in large number, since their votes are not clearly cast for any particular issue or set of issues.

3. Rational Ignorance and political Beliefs

At this level we should note that, the theory of rational ignorance and rational irrationality does not predict that voters (citizens) will avoid acquiring political knowledge entirely. These theories imply that voters will acquire little or no knowledge for voting's purpose. The most powerful determinant of political knowledge is that it should entertain people to be effective.

Political ignorance is mostly compared with "stupidity", But in this work we could proof that also highly intelligent voters can be rationally choose to apply for little information, that mean devote little or no effort to acquiring political knowledge. That is rational and the dilemma we try to explain at this part is to also to show why people can rationally choose to vote, while at the same time remaining ignorant of basic political information.

The economist Anthony Downs formulated the theory of rational ignorance back in the 1950s. Like written bellow, an individual voter has virtually no chance to influence the outcome of election; the probability is less than 1 in 100 Million in the case of modern US presidential election. According to this knowledge a result of such daunting odds, the incentive to accumulate a needed political knowledge is vanishingly small. The informed electorate is a public good the provision of which is subject to the collective action problem which arises when consumers of good do not have to help pay for its provision in order to enjoy its benefits. Honestly, only professional politicians and those who value political knowledge have an incentive to lean significant amount of it. It will be irrational to acquiring extensive political knowledge only because of election, because that will be costly high and require more than just being getting the information. It is important to recognize that this logic is that it applies just as readily to highly altruistic and civic-minded citizens as to narrowly self-interested ones. Even a 100 percent altruistic person - someone who always chooses to prioritize the welfare of others over her own whenever the two conflict - would not rationally devote much of her time to acquiring political information for the sake of casting an informed vote. (econ.as.nyu.edu)

We cannot definitely know that the rational ignorance hypothesis is correct. But the available evidence strongly supports it. Otherwise, it is difficult to explain the fact that political knowledge levels have remained roughly stable at very low levels for decades, despite massive increases in education levels and in the availability of information through the media and now the internet.

Derek Parfit has demonstrated theoretically, and Edlin, Gelman, and Kaplan have supported with empirical evidence, the decision to vote is rational so long as the voter perceives a significant difference between candidates and cares even slightly about the welfare of fellow citizens, as well as his own. A simple calculation, derived from Parfit's analysis shows why this is true.

Assume that Uv = expected utility of voting; Cv = cost of voting; and D=expected

And because voter´s ballot only has 1 in 100 million probabilities to change the outcome, that voter value the welfare of his fellow citizens an average of 1000 time less than his own. (econ.as.nyu.edu) that bring to this equation:

$D*(300 \text{ million}/1000)/(100 \text{ million}) - Cv = Uv$. (The Utlity of Voting Equation)

According to the example of econ.as.nyu If we assume that Cv is \$10 (a reasonable proxy for the cost of voting) and that D is \$5000 (this can incorporate monetary equivalents of noneconomic benefits as well as actual income increases), then Uv equals \$5, a small but real positive expected utility. Voters do not precisely calculate like this, but they might make an intuitive judgment incorporating very rough estimates of D and C. the fact that voting is a low-cost, low-benefit activity ensures that there is little benefit to engaging in precise calculations such as these, so voters might rationally choose to go with a default option of voting and forego any detailed analysis. (John Aldrich *American Journal of Political Science* 37) The cost of the latter could itself easily outweigh the benefit of saving time and money on voting. (Terry M. Moe 1980)

The Paper of nyu also use one of the best example to show the Utility of acquiring political information for Voting Purpose and they proceed like this: Assume that Upi = the utility of acquiring sufficient political information to make a "correct" decision and Cpi = the cost of acquiring political information. Thus:

D*(300 million/1000)/(100 million) – Cpi = Upi. (*The Utility of Acquiring Political Information For Voting Purposes*)

Example: If we conservatively estimate Cpi at $100 by assuming that the voter need only expend 10 hours to acquire and learn the necessary information while suffering opportunity costs of just $10 per hour, then the magnitude of D would have to be nearly seven times greater--$33,333 per citizen--in order for the voter to choose to make the necessary expenditure on information acquisition. It is unlikely that many otherwise ignorant voters will perceive such an enormous potential difference between the opposing candidates as to invest even the equivalent of $100 in information acquisition. And this theoretical prediction is consistent with the empirical observation that most citizens in fact know very little about politics and public policy, but do vote.

NYU Paper also shows that, if voter does not care about the national welfare, but about other factors such as their racial or ethnic group (US presidential election of 2008). Voter may believe that that candidates´ policy (Obama policies) will benefit some groups (blacks) more than others. We can calculate the utility increase to whatever groups the voter does care about and discount it by the extent to which the elector cares about them less about himself, and by the likelihood of her vote being decisive. Because the result number is greater than the cost of voting, it will be rational to go to the polls. The cost of acquiring information is remain likely to make being well informed irrational. The result of this will than bring us to this next equation:

The Utility of Voting, Assuming Unequal Valuation of Different Groups' Welfare
D*((250 million/1000) + 50 million/200)/(100 million) – Cv = Uv.

According to all equations and we could be sure that a normal rational voter will only need to use his intuition and sense apply for knowledge about policies and then make a good vote decision. All rational people use those intuition before they vote, bit we could keep in mind that rational ignorance is mostly an alternative, because the cost to acquire information is more expensive that the benefit of this.

Because Voter is not ready to apply for information before they go to the polls, politician may abuse this failed knowledge to vote some policies that are not favorable to voters. That effect of fiscal illusion that politicians have is a pretty biggest problem and the reason that do not encourage voter to vote. The next part of this paper will try to build a model that may reduce that fiscal illusion.

3.1. Policies that might reduce fiscal illusion

The attractiveness of financing spending by debt issue to the elected politicians should be obvious. Borrowing allows spending to be made that will yield immediate political payoffs without the incurring of any immediate political cost.
—James Buchanan (1984)

First of all we should try to define what fiscal illusion is. That word fiscal illusion was already mentioned on this paper directly and indirectly. But to make sure at this level that that clears is, I will try to give a short definition of this term. Fiscal illusion is a theory of government expenditure developed by Amilcare Puviani. It suggest that when government revenues are unobserved or not fully observed by taxpayers then the cost of government is perceived to be less expensive than it actually is. Fiscal Illusion is mentioned as an explanation whythe local taxpayers are under the mistaken perception that the grant is to local government and not, in fact, to them.

Eileen Norcross and Frederic Saubet from Marcatus Center (George Mason University) have some policy recommendation that could reduce fiscal illusion. In their paper they take the example of the State of New-Jersey as one of the most overburdened State with legislation and complex system taxation. The two economists propose four solutions to that problem: 1. Create an Effective constitutional Rules to constrain Spending (Colorado´s Taxpayers Bill of Rights TABOR); For example, if inflation is 3 percent a year and population growth is stable, government can only increase spending by three percent in nominal terms. If tax revenue increased more than 3 percent in that same year, the surplus is rebated to taxpayers. If Government want for example to spend beyond, they must ask citizens through ballot measures (i.e., citizen initiatives) This policy could automatically forces government to reduce taxation to the level that reflect the amount citizens wish to spend. Those direct Democracy force transparency in public policy. Thos kind of policy creates an explicit contractual relationship between taxpayers and elected officials, taxpayers may have a clearer picture of how funds are spend.

The second Solution is to reform public expenditure by using those constitutional rule like TABOR as a constrain against the growth of public spending over time. And the third and last solution is to create a Tax environment that Favors Growth (Broad Bases and Low Rates) and the last solution is introducing competition to local Government.

Those policies could probably help to reduce fiscal illusion, but the problem is to make a differentiation between fiscal illusion and tax spends. The model bellow is at the moment the only one that could really help to reduce fiscal illusion.

4. Conclusion

Bryan Caplan said "*information is a good like other*". It cost and that cost can sometime be higher that a benefit cost. In the whole paper, I trying to show why people prefer being rational ignorant, try to find out the origin of this ignorance that rational is, the effect of this ignorance, that is sometime called rational irrationality. Even if economists believe that voter ignorance remain a serious problem for democracy, it is important to carefully work through the direction of the effect. (Caplan, 1999) To reduce effectively that problem of ration ignorance elector could maybe more work on transparency by election campaign and make all their policies clear for voters. The politic arena don't have definite rules and every candidate use his intelligence to manipulate the population, particularly those who are not pretty informed. We have seen in the long of this paper, that issues are not only connected to information application, but also on much different kind of biases. People have believe and convictions and they, and they do also have different kind of issue, depending on their social group, or their believe, all this have effect on the perception of rationality. In the Akerlof lemons model, to take the canonical example, informed sellers and uninformed buyers leads the use car market to think. Buyers realize that they are unable to judge product quality, and therefore become more reluctant to buy. In The same way of view, if political informed or insider really knows more about program quality than voters, voters´ rational response is, in effect to say "When in doubt, vote no". in equilibrium, then asymmetric political information tend to make government smaller, not bigger. (Bryan Caplan, 1999)

The dominance of interest in politics as a predictor of political knowledge also highlights the dangers of rational irrationality. If most citizens who acquire political information do so primarily for reasons other than truth-seeking, there is little reason to expect them to analyze it in a rational or unbiased way. (econ.as.nyu)

Rational Ignorance is only an imperfect representation of the reality. Is not easy to resolve this problem, because of much different kind of reasons: Economic cannot explain all people behavior. Everyone do have his own behavior than other one, the same could be applied in the rational ignorance. The standard economic theories try to use the theory of homo economicus define the person as rational and selfish, someone that only act, when he see his interest. That could be applied to the rational ignorance theory, but this model is not universal, because person may have other motivations like reciprocity, or could be altruist or only stupid. From all this reasons, is pretty difficult to find solution against rational ignorance.

Reference:

Caplan, Bryan (2003), Rational Irrationality, the Encyclopedia of Public Choice, PP 795-797
Buchanan, James M,; Wagner Richard E. (1997). Democracy in Deficit: The political Legacy of Lord Keynes. New York: Academic Press. Retrived 2011.01.19

Caplan, Bryan. 2000. "Rational Irrationality: A Framework for the Neoclassical-Behavioral Debate." *Eastern Economic Journal* 26, pp.191-211.

Caplan, Bryan. 2001b. "Rational Irrationality and the Microfoundations of Political Failure." *Public Choice* 107, pp.311-331.

Caplan, Bryan. 2001c. "Rational Ignorance versus Rational Irrationality." *Kyklos* 54, pp.3-26.
National Survey of Public Knowledge of Welfare Reform and the Federal Budget. Kaiser Family Foundation and Harvard University, January 12 1995, #1001.

Olson, Mancur. "Big Bills Left on the Sidewalk: Why Some Nations are Rich and Others are Poor." Journal of Economic Perspectives, Spring 1996, 3-24.

Olson, Mancur. *The Rise and Decline of Nations: Economic Growth, Stagflation and Social Rigidities.* New Haven: Yale University Press, 1982.

Olson, Mancur. *The Logic of Collective Action: Public Goods and the Theory of Groups.* Cambridge: Harvard University Press, 1965.

Caplan, Bryan. forthcoming. "The Logic of Collective Belief." *Rationality and Society.*
Caplan, Bryan. 2002. "Systematically Biased Beliefs About Economics: Robust Evidence of Judgmental Anomalies from the Survey of Americans and Economists on the Economy." *Economic Journal* 112, pp.1-26.

Josh Billings, Caruth and Ehrlich. 1988 P. 205

"Witchcraft." Britannica CD. Version 97. Encyclopaedia Britannica, Inc., 1997.
Wittman, Donald. *The Myth of Democratic Failure: Why Political Institutions are Efficient.* Chicago: University of Chicago Press, 1995.

Wittman, Donald. "Why Democracies Produce Efficient Results." Journal of Political Economy, December 1989, 1395-1424.

Wittman, Donald. *The Myth of Democratic Failure: Why Political Institutions are Efficient.* Chicago: University of Chicago Press, 1995.

Wittman, Donald. "Why Democracies Produce Efficient Results." Journal of Political Economy, December 1989, 1395-1424. Wittman, Donald. 1995. *The Myth of Democratic Failure: Why Political Institutions are Efficient.* (Chicago: University of Chicago Press).

Akerlof, George, and William Dickens. 1982. The Economic Consequences of Cognitive Dissonance. *American Economic Review* 72, pp.307-19.

Anthony Downs, *An Economic Theory of Democracy*, (New York: Harper & Row, 1957), ch. 13

William H. Riker and Peter Ordeshook, "A Theory of the Calculus of Voting," *American Political Science Review* 62 (1968): 25-42. Andrew Gelman, et al., "What is the Probability that Your Vote Will Make a Difference? *Economic Inquiry* (forthcoming), available at http://www.stat.columbia.edu/~gelman/research/published/probdecisive2.pdf. Gelman, et al, estimate that the chance of decisiveness in the 2008 presidential election varied from 1 in 10 million in a few small states, to 1 in 100 million in large states such as California (Ibid., 9-10).

Olson, *Logic of Collective Action*; Russell Hardin, *Collective Action*, (Chicago: University of Chicago Press, 1982).

For studies showing little or no increase in political knowledge over time, see Delli Carpini and Keeter, *What Americans Know About Politics and Why It Matters*, 62–134; Eric R.A.N. Smith, *The Unchanging American Voter* (Berkeley: University of California Press, 1989); Stephen E. Bennett, "'Know-Nothings' Revisited: The Meaning of Political Ignorance Today," *Social Science Quarterly* 69 (1988): 476; Stephen E. Bennett, "Know-Nothings Revisited Again," *Political Behavior* 18 (1996): 219; Stephen E. Bennett, "Trends in Americans' Political Information, 1967–87," *American Politics Quarterly* 17 (1989): 422; Michael X. Delli Carpini and Scott Keeter, "Stability and Change in the U.S. Public's Knowledge of Politics," *Public Opinion Quarterly* 55 (1991): 583; but see Scott L. Althaus, *Collective Preferences in Democratic Politics* (New York: Cambridge University Press, 2003), 215 which found a very small increase in knowledge when comparing the 1980-88 period to 1990-98. The increase show in Althaus' study is extremely low (from an average of 52% correct answers in the earlier period to 54% in the later one), and may be an artifact of the particular questions studied.

Derek Parfit, Reasons and Persons (Oxford: Clarendon Press, 1984), 73-75.

Aaron Edlin, Andrew Gelman, and Noah Kaplan, "Voting as a Rational Choice: Why and How People Vote to Improve the Well-Being of Others," Rationality and Society, 19 (2007): 293-314

This assumption of modest altruism is plausible. Empirical evidence provides some support for this conjecture. Americans spend some three percent of their household income on charity. See Arthur Brooks, *Who Really Cares? America's Charity Divide*, (New York: Basic Books, 2006), 3; Richard B. McKenzie, "Was it a Decade of Greed?" *Public Interest* 27 (1992), 91-96. This is very likely a far greater sum than - judging by survey evidence of the results - individual voters spend on acquiring political information.

See, e.g., Brian Barry, *Economists, Sociologists, and Democracy*, (Chicago: University of Chicago Press, 2nd ed. 1978).

See Terry M. Moe, *The Organization of Interests*, (Chicago: University of Chicago Press, 1980), pp. 70-72

John Aldrich, "Rational Choice and Turnout." *American Journal of Political Science* 37: 246-78

http://newjersey.mercatus.org/policy-recommendations/ (August 28th, 2010)
http://econ.as.nyu.edu/docs/IO/16670/Somin_2_20101213.pdf (July (July 30th, 2010)
http://home.sprynet.com/~owl1/irrationality.htm (August 15th, 2010)
http://www.cato.org/pubs/journal/cj29n3/cj29n3-6.pdf (August 15th, 2010)
http://www.independent.org/pdf/working_papers/04_logic.pdf (July 29th, 2010)
http://www.cato.org/pubs/journal/cj29n3/cj29n3-6.pdf (August 26th, 2010)